Milestones

For Mom

A Celebration Journal for Moms

This Journal Belongs to:

_____

Copyright © 2019 Ambi Shantay

All rights reserved.

www.ambishantay.com

ISBN: 978-1-7342176-2-9

This journal is for every woman who has assisted in molding, shaping, and nurturing a child of her own. Motherhood is indeed the greatest gift I have ever been given; and I reap its rewards every single day! Some of us are more seasoned in this calling, while others (like myself) still have a long way to go. My desire is that this journal goes with you on your journey through parenthood. Record every milestone, every moment, every memory that you want to remain close to your heart, from birth to adulthood. You can also utilize this journal as a creative space to save keepsakes and photos throughout the years.

Our children grow so fast. One day, all we will have are these precious memories to reflect upon. Throughout this book, you will find reflections from some of my friends. These ladies are different races, different ages, in different geographic locations; yet the one thing that brings us together is the bond of motherhood. You've been afforded a beautiful opportunity, my sister- one that many hope for. I pray you continue making memories with your family and your journal, memories that will stay with you forever and ever....in Jesus Name.

Amen

Milestone

A significant event, Occasion, or Stage in the life, Progress, or Development of an individual

My Milestone Moment

It's the milestone moments that sometimes stop me in my tracks. Every accomplishment they do throughout their lives (large or small) becomes yours and often I'm just in awe of these human beings that my husband and I created. I look at my older children now and I think - "We made them. They are pretty awesome adults."
-Roshelle Howell Parker

Date _____

On this day, I Celebrate

_____
_____
_____
_____
_____
_____
_____
_____
_____
_____
_____
_____
_____
_____
_____
_____
_____

Date _____

On this day, I Celebrate

_____
_____
_____
_____
_____
_____
_____
_____
_____
_____
_____
_____
_____
_____
_____
_____
_____

My Milestone Moment

Seeing them smile. My heart is so full knowing that my children (6, 4, 8 months) have so much happiness in their hearts to make them smile.
-Chasity Buchanan Lane

Date_____

On this day, I Celebrate

_____
_____
_____
_____
_____
_____
_____
_____
_____
_____
_____
_____
_____
_____
_____
_____
_____
_____

My Milestone Moment

My favorite part of mother hood is, even on the days I have felt that I let them down or I'm not good enough for them, they always seem to tell me they love me and that I am a great mom. And even on days when all I do is yell, there they are with arms wide open for a snuggle or a hug.
-Daisy Page

Celebrate

Date _____

On this day, I Celebrate

_____
_____
_____
_____
_____
_____
_____
_____
_____
_____
_____
_____
_____
_____
_____
_____
_____

My Milestone Moment

Hands down watching them grow into their own little people and knowing that you were a big part of that. Mine is 16 and it's so hard having to let go a little at a time knowing that soon he will have to take the ropes. Fearing the "big world" for him and knowing you can't be there for every moment that's hard but making sure they know you're always here when they do need you. And hoping that everything you instilled in them sticks. Just knowing that little human was something you created and something God picked you to be a part of.

-Alex Wheeler

Date _____

On this day, I Celebrate

My Milestone Moment

Being their witness. Just truly seeing another person and witnessing the parts of their lives that no one else will ever see. Like the way they looked at 3 a.m. when the rest of the world was sound asleep, and it is just you that your child needed. Or those preciously fleeting first few weeks of life when you witness every change from the rapid filling out of sweet baby cheeks to the gazes that become more focused each day. Things that neither they, nor anyone else, will remember are held in my heart. I have the privilege of witnessing the lives of 5 amazing individuals, and treasuring each nuance of their existence.
-Laura Henderson Bates

Date _____

On this day, I Celebrate

Celebrate

Date _____

On this day, I Celebrate

My Milestone Moment

My favorite part of being a mom is knowing what a blessing it is to be a mom. Knowing that I get to help this little person grow, learn, and become something more. It's understanding that although an experience is old to us, it's new to them, and looking at things through their eyes.
-Natasha Garrett Miles

Date _____

On this day, I Celebrate

_____
_____
_____
_____
_____
_____
_____
_____
_____
_____
_____
_____
_____
_____
_____
_____
_____
_____

My Milestone Moment

To see and know God actually sent these gifts of life, beauty, and intelligence just for you and to you is a miracle in itself. The daily journey; adventures; highs and lows; development; changes; and learning are all experiences for both me as a Mother and my children. We have daily routines and affirmations that assist us throughout our day and help us evolve daily. My two daughters are still so young and little, yet wise and mature beyond their years. I have placed crowns upon their heads as their Queen Mother. I prayed for them before I even knew they existed and I pray for them now. That will never stop. The legacy certainly continues.
-A.K Johnson

Date _____

On this day, I Celebrate

Celebrate

Date _____

On this day, I Celebrate

_____

_____

_____

_____

_____

_____

_____

_____

_____

_____

_____

_____

_____

_____

_____

My Milestone Moment

Just to hear... "Mama, I have something to tell you! Mama, can we take a ride, I need to talk!"
It gives me so much joy in knowing that THEY TRUST ME..THEY KNOW I LOVE THEM.. I THANK GOD FOR THAT EVERYDAY!
They never go to bed without saying "I love you..." Even when I'm away, I'll receive a text or something!
-Cole Robb

Date _____

On this day, I Celebrate

My Milestone Moment

For me, it's seeing life through their eyes and watching them grow into productive citizens who will eventually have a family of their own. Knowing I have a hand in how they will flourish in this world is major.
-Autumn Prather

Date _____

On this day, I Celebrate

Celebrate

Date _____

On this day, I Celebrate

_____
_____
_____
_____
_____
_____
_____
_____
_____
_____
_____
_____
_____
_____
_____
_____
_____

My Milestone Moment

To see their faces light up when they've conquered things, the openness to share their concerns & look to me to have all the answers, their caring & nurturing spirit to others!!!! This is what I reflect on when I'm having a rough day
-Latosha McKinley

Date _____

On this day, I Celebrate

My Milestone Moment

Mine would be my daughter (at age 5 or 6) telling me to "go to your room and do your Bible study. And don't come back out until there is more of Jesus than mommy." I laughed so hard.
-Amanda Bradley

Date _____

On this day, I Celebrate

Celebrate

Date _____

On this day, I Celebrate

_____
_____
_____
_____
_____
_____
_____
_____
_____
_____
_____
_____
_____
_____
_____
_____
_____

My Milestone Moment

My favorite part of being a Mother is just seeing God work in his life. Especially after I was told I would never be a Mother. After Eli was born early, the doctors told me my baby would be slow in every area of his life. Because I know who and whose I am, I spoke life over my baby. He started crawling/walking early. He is so smart that teachers want to advance him to a higher class. He loves our prayer time
-T. Fleming

Date _____

On this day, I Celebrate

My Milestone Moment

I have a whole list of things but mostly the small things make it all worth it. Waking them up in the morning and getting morning hugs. Picking them up from school and hearing all about their day. I'm so grateful and do not take motherhood lightly as I know it's truly an honor and privilege to be blessed with children.
-D. Hall-Greene

Date _____

On this day, I Celebrate

Celebrate

Date _____

On this day, I Celebrate

My Milestone Moment

My boys are silly!! My youngest does this funny walk and then looks at me to laugh at him. My oldest loves *Frozen* and I love when he sings with Ana.

-H. M Harris

Date _____

On this day, I Celebrate

_____
_____
_____
_____
_____
_____
_____
_____
_____
_____
_____
_____
_____
_____
_____
_____
_____
_____

My Milestone Moment

My favorite part about being a mom is all the small moments that fill your heart instantly with joy and love. It's those little hugs, the slobbery kisses and big laughs. Silly dances and watching them have so much fun playing. It's the pride from them accomplishing anything you know they've worked to learn. It's the eye contact from your toddler for acceptance. The blanket cuddles and songs. Them holding your hand. Them just needing and loving mommy. It's just all the little moments that add up to fill and complete your heart every single day.
-Tavia Smith

Date _____

On this day, I Celebrate

_____
_____
_____
_____
_____
_____
_____
_____
_____
_____
_____
_____
_____
_____
_____
_____
_____

Celebrate

Date _____

On this day, I Celebrate

My Milestone Moment

Seeing them acting and participating in life better than I had ever dreamed of or hoped for.
-W. Dupree

Date _____

On this day, I Celebrate

_____
_____
_____
_____
_____
_____
_____
_____
_____
_____
_____
_____
_____
_____
_____

My Milestone Moment

I was told that I would never have kids. For those that struggle with fertility the intense emotions and physical effects of hormones that you have to use can take its toll in every area of your life. But when you get to hold your child for the first time...none of that other stuff ever matters again. Life is precious and I thank God for the honor to be a mother to a Baby Boy!
-C. Scott

Date _____

On this day, I Celebrate

Celebrate

Date _____

On this day, I Celebrate

_____
_____
_____
_____
_____
_____
_____
_____
_____
_____
_____
_____
_____
_____
_____
_____
_____
_____
_____

My Milestone Moment

One of my joys of motherhood is becoming a grandmother and seeing my daughter no longer as just a daughter, but as a mother
-S.Oglesby

Date _____

On this day, I Celebrate

_____
_____
_____
_____
_____
_____
_____
_____
_____
_____
_____
_____
_____
_____
_____

My Milestone Moment

I have many...one of them is simply when "they get it." When they understand what it is that is being conveyed. My daughter had some friends over. One friend stated "y'all are lucky, y'all have a big house." I was in another room; but I heard my daughter reply, "We are lucky because we have a house." That touched me because she "got it." We try to impart in our kids gratefulness, appreciation, thankfulness and so on. It's just God loving on us. So when I see or hear those "life lessons" being manifested through their young lives, that gives me joy.

-L. Bell

Date _____

On this day, I Celebrate

Celebrate

Date _____

On this day, I Celebrate

My Milestone Moment

No matter if it's by breast or bottle, I enjoy the look and connection I feel and see when my daughter is enjoying her meal. The sounds she makes and her smile lets me know I'm doing something right
-S. Ferguson

Date _____

On this day, I Celebrate

My Milestone Moment

To see that God trusted me with this precious gift of a daughter!
-D. Solomon

Date _____

On this day, I Celebrate

Celebrate

Date _____

On this day, I Celebrate

My Milestone Moment

My girls are 35 and 31; and they still believe mama can fix anything. And they still tell me that
-C. Eules-Curry

Date _____

On this day, I Celebrate

My Milestone Moment

My baby is 39. People tell us all the time we look like sisters and even more she is my best friend. Our later years have been so much better because we grew to love and respect each other more each day. We travel and share every aspect of life. And most of all, our connection is so strong, one is picking up the phone as the other is calling. God has brought us a long way!
-C. Gist

Date _____

On this day, I Celebrate

Celebrate

Date _____

On this day, I Celebrate

_____

_____

_____

_____

_____

_____

_____

_____

_____

_____

_____

_____

_____

_____

_____

_____

_____

_____

My Milestone Moment

For me... although my baby is only 6 months old, the bond that we have is amazing!! When I walk in the room his face lights up! And there have been days where I just wasn't feeling good and it's like He knows it! He looks at me as if to say "You gone be ok mama" or he will lay his head on my chest or shoulder and smile at me... it's like He's loving me back to health!!!

-M. Demoss

Date _____

On this day, I Celebrate

My Milestone Moment

It's the hugs, love, care and concern when they can feel or see something is bothering you. It's the wasted groceries because they fixed breakfast without asking you what you wanted to eat! It's memories we shared with my Mom like helping to make the corn bread dressing for Thanksgiving. About making your own memories after you lose someone precious.
-L.Slusher

Date _____

On this day, I Celebrate

Celebrate

Date _____

On this day, I Celebrate

_____
_____
_____
_____
_____
_____
_____
_____
_____
_____
_____
_____
_____
_____
_____
_____
_____
_____
_____
_____

My Milestone Moment

My favorite is when we slow down and are just together. No matter what is - sitting, napping, watching a great movie, relaxing, cuddling, talking, asking & answering questions, dancing, singing real LOUD, telling jokes, being awesome, playing with the dog, cooking dinner and all the silly (and sometimes gross) things boys do...

It really doesn't matter the activity as long as we are within arm's reach of each other.

-L. Covington-Johnson

Date _____

On this day, I Celebrate

_____

_____

_____

_____

_____

_____

_____

_____

_____

_____

_____

_____

_____

_____

_____

_____

_____

_____

_____

My Milestone Moment

My 9 yr. old son loves it when I tuck him in at night and we tell each other "I love You to the moon and back" and we then grab each other's noses. It's something that's just shared between him and me. I cherish each moment.

-K. Dean

Date _____

On this day, I Celebrate

Celebrate

Date _____

On this day, I Celebrate

My Milestone Moment

In no order if importance...1) Hearing their excited voices call me first to tell me something good that just happened to them. 2) having received a phone call/letter of appreciation (after they were grown) thanking us for all we did for them while in school and in college. Thankful that they ended college with no debt or other bills. "Looking at my friends I realize how much you did and it is appreciated" 3) hearing them tell "momma and daddy" stories to their friends. It never gets old, no matter how old your babies are (mine happen to be 41 and 38). 4) asking for my advice

-A. Whiteside

Date _____

On this day, I Celebrate

_____
_____
_____
_____
_____
_____
_____
_____
_____
_____
_____
_____
_____
_____
_____
_____

My Milestone Moment

When my son says, "Mama you know everything." He doesn't realize I'm still learning.
-J. Jennings

Date _____

On this day, I Celebrate

Celebrate

Date _____

On this day, I Celebrate

_____
_____
_____
_____
_____
_____
_____
_____
_____
_____
_____
_____
_____
_____
_____
_____
_____
_____
_____
_____

My Milestone Moment

I have so many from all four of my children, (20, 19, 10 & 9) but my only daughter (10 years old) just melts my heart daily with her hugs, compliments, kisses and encouragement. She never fails to say to me, "Mommy, you're so beautiful. I want to be just like you when I grow up. As a matter of fact, save all of your shoes, clothes and jewelry for me so I can wear them when I'm grown!" Even when I feel like I've not done enough for them, one of "my gifts" never fail to remind me of how much they love me and that it's OK. I just LOVE them!!!

-G. Hayslett-Isaac

Date _____

On this day, I Celebrate

Date _____

On this day, I Celebrate

Celebrate

Date _____

On this day, I Celebrate

Date _____

On this day, I Celebrate

Date _____

On this day, I Celebrate

_____
_____
_____
_____
_____
_____
_____
_____
_____
_____
_____
_____
_____
_____
_____
_____
_____

Celebrate

Date _____

On this day, I Celebrate

_____
_____
_____
_____
_____
_____
_____
_____
_____
_____
_____
_____
_____
_____
_____
_____

Date _____

On this day, I Celebrate

_____
_____
_____
_____
_____
_____
_____
_____
_____
_____
_____
_____
_____
_____
_____
_____

Date _____

On this day, I Celebrate

Celebrate

Date _____

On this day, I Celebrate

Date _____

On this day, I Celebrate

_____
_____
_____
_____
_____
_____
_____
_____
_____
_____
_____
_____
_____
_____
_____
_____

Date _____

On this day, I Celebrate

_____
_____
_____
_____
_____
_____
_____
_____
_____
_____
_____
_____
_____
_____
_____
_____
_____
_____
_____

Celebrate

Date _____

On this day, I Celebrate

Date _____

On this day, I Celebrate

_____
_____
_____
_____
_____
_____
_____
_____
_____
_____
_____
_____
_____
_____
_____
_____
_____
_____

Date _____

On this day, I Celebrate

Celebrate

Date _____

On this day, I Celebrate

Date _____

On this day, I Celebrate

_____
_____
_____
_____
_____
_____
_____
_____
_____
_____
_____
_____
_____
_____
_____
_____
_____
_____
_____
_____

Date _____

On this day, I Celebrate

Made in the USA
Columbia, SC
13 February 2021